Sticker Maths for School

Written by David Kremer
Illustrated by Ian Cunliffe

Ladybird

Size and ordering

Adventure on Animal Island

Find the sticker rocks to make a path to Animal Island. The rocks are ordered from the **smallest** to the **biggest.**

A feather, a shell and a coconut are under a tree. Find the stickers and put them in order from the **lightest** to the **heaviest.**

Find the stickers with these numbers on and put them in order from the **smallest** to the **largest.**

20 12 4 0 9 16 19

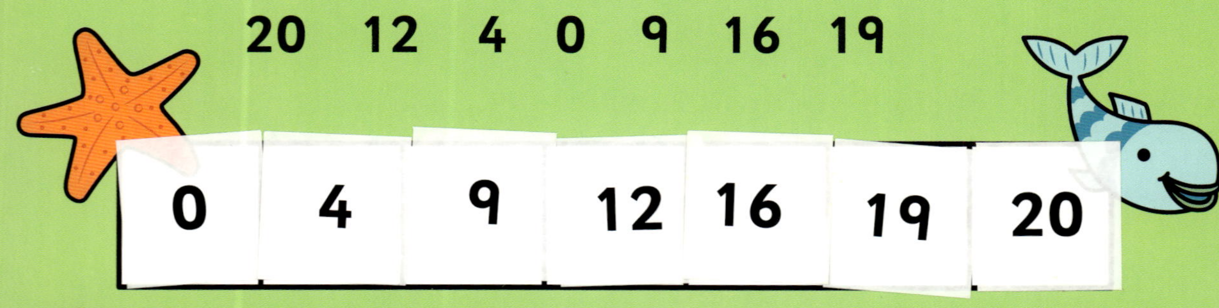

The cheeky monkeys who live on Animal Island have made some banana-flavoured milkshakes for everyone!

Put the glasses in order from the **fullest** to the **emptiest.**

Complete the sums.

Adding to ten

__ + 5 = 10

6 + __ = 10

__ + 7 = 10

0 + __ = 10

4 + __ = 10

__ + 3 = 10

__ + 2 = 10

9 + __ = 10

Subtracting from ten

10 - 9 = __

10 - 6 = __

10 - __ = 7

__ - 8 = 2

__ - 1 = 9

10 - __ = 8

10 - 0 = __

Time

The old clock shop

Match the correct word stickers to the times on the clocks.

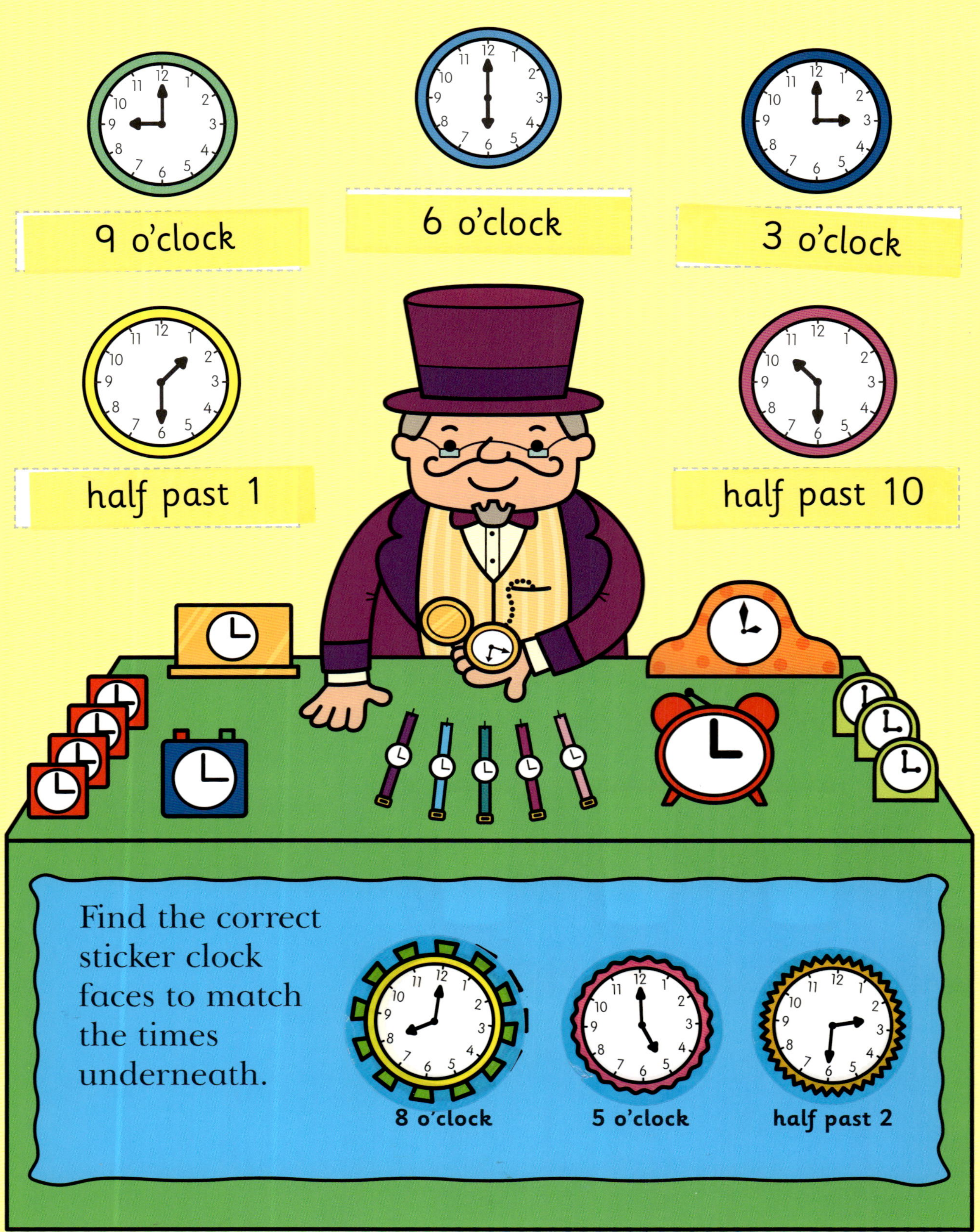

Find the correct sticker clock faces to match the times underneath.

These are the times that the clockmaker's family get up in the morning. Write them in order from the **earliest** to the **latest**.

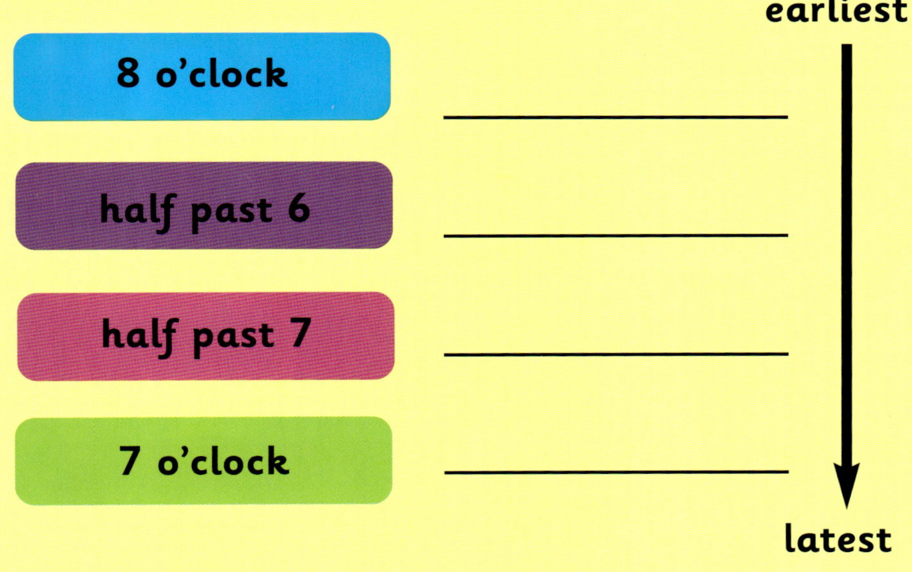

Draw hands on each clock to show the time.

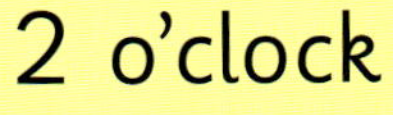

2 o'clock

3 o'clock

half past 5

half past 1

12 o'clock

What time is half an hour after 6 o'clock?

____

What time is 1 hour before 3 o'clock?

____

What time is half an hour before 8 o'clock?

____

What time is half an hour after half past 10?

____

What time is 1 hour before 1 o'clock?

____

What time is 2 hours after 10 o'clock?

____

Money

The school fête

Find the correct sticker coins to make the exact money needed to buy each delicious treat.

apple 15p

pizza 55p

orange juice 18p

jacket potato 74p

spaghetti bolognese £2.45

Match the sticker bags to the amount of money each child should have.

Here are two coins. How much more money will make exactly £1?

Stick any coins you haven't used here. What do they add up to?

Patterns and sequences

Patterns at the palace

Find the stickers to complete the sequences.

Use the leftover stickers to make some more patterns of your own.

Fill in the blanks in the following number sequences.

1. 2 4 __ 8 __ 12 14

2. __ 10 15 __ 25 __ 35

3. 12 11 __ 9 __ 7 6

4. 22 __ 20 __ 18 17 __

5. 10 __ 30 __ 50 60 __

6. __ 98 99 __ 101 __ __

7. 100 ___ 300 ___ 500 ___ 700

8. __ 6 9 __ 15 __ 21

9. 1 2 4 __ 16 __ 64

Adding and subtracting

Let's play some games!

Find the missing stickers of games and toys. Then read the instructions and play the game with a friend.

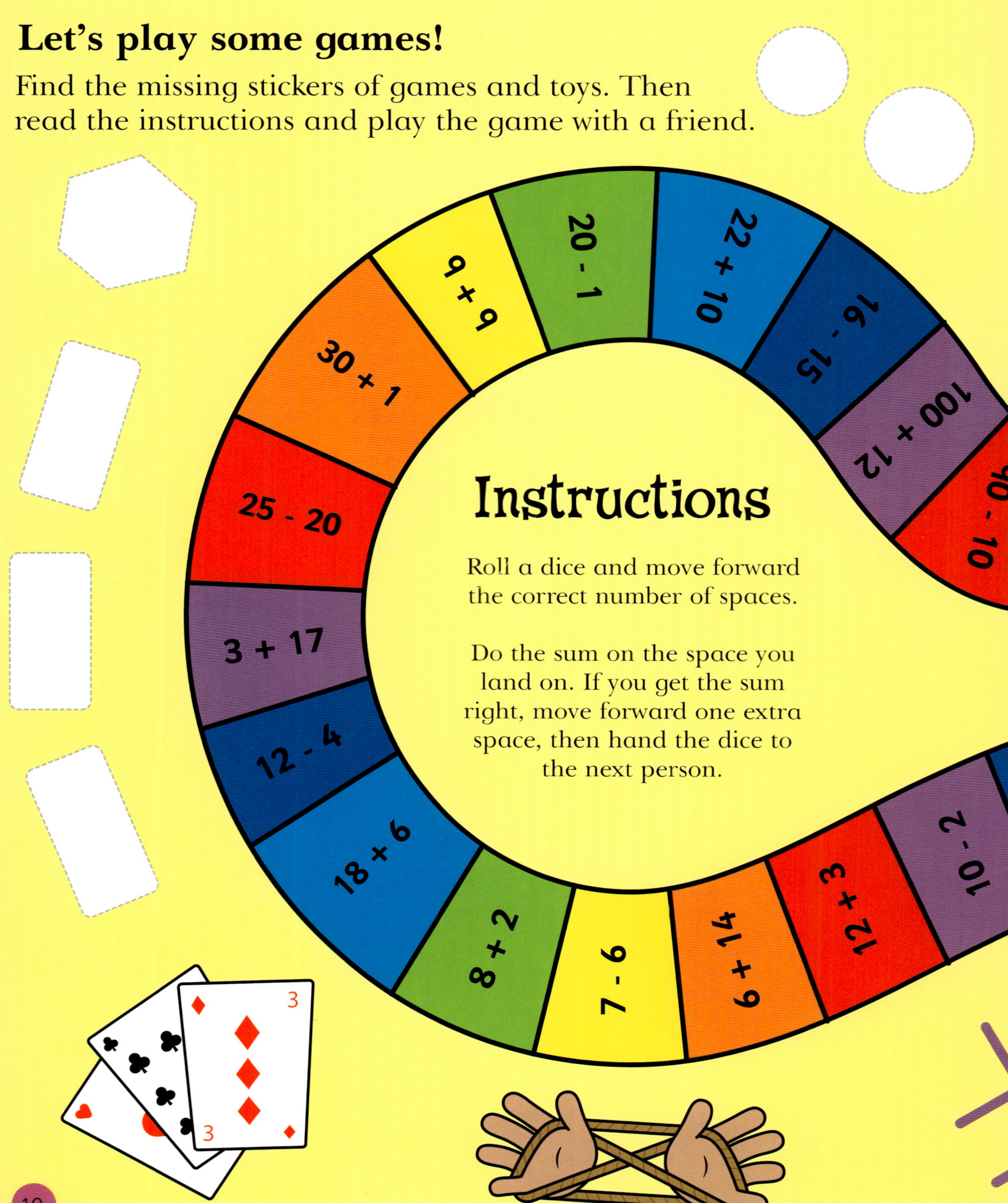

Instructions

Roll a dice and move forward the correct number of spaces.

Do the sum on the space you land on. If you get the sum right, move forward one extra space, then hand the dice to the next person.

Leapfrog shapes!

Draw a line to show a path through the shapes to get home. You can only step on a shape that has more corners than the shape that you are already on.

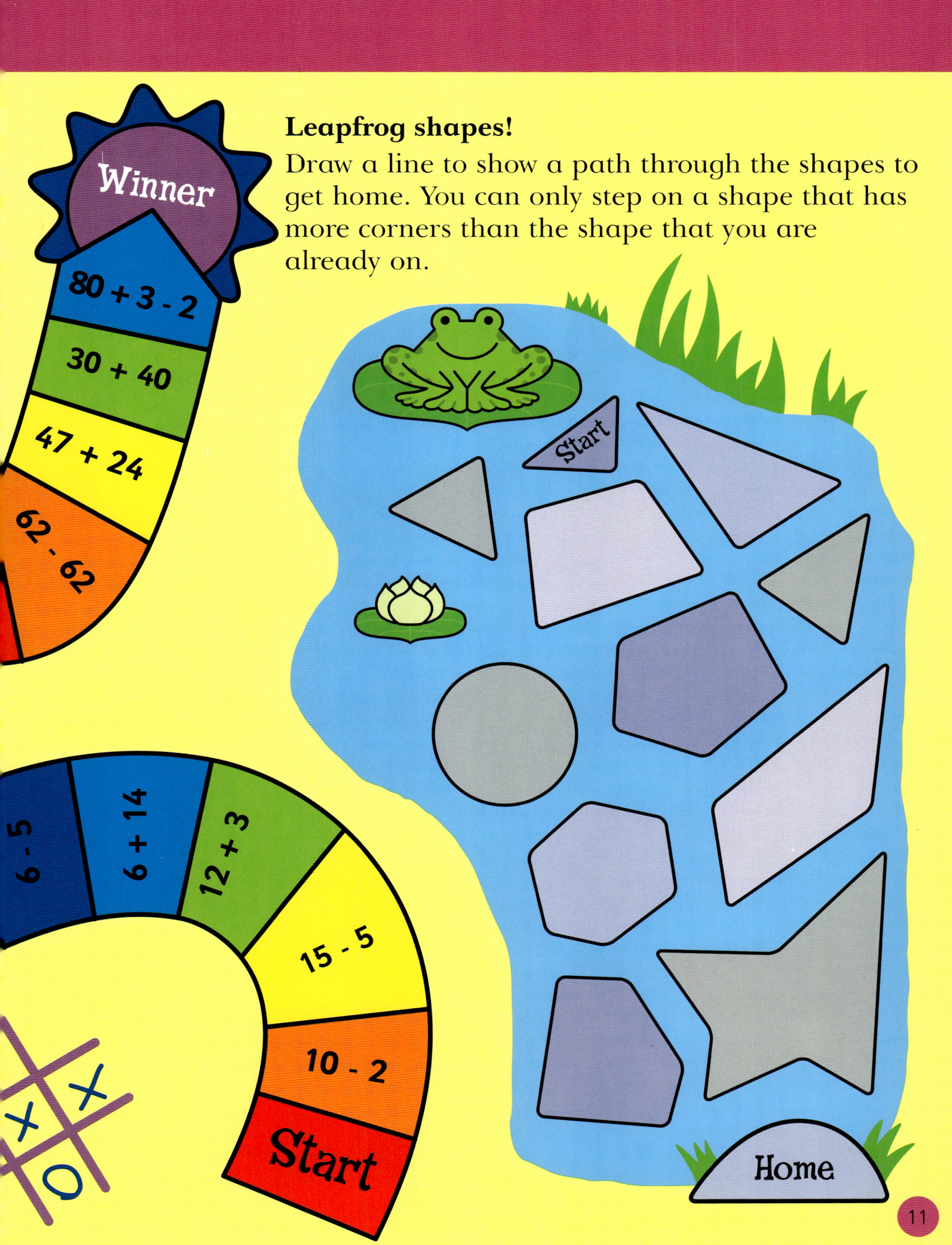

Multiplying and dividing

Chocolate challenge

Find the missing chocolate stickers and do the sums.

5 blocks x 2 rows = 10 blocks altogether. 5 x 2 = 10

4 blocks x 2 rows = ____ blocks altogether. 4 x 2 = ____

3 blocks x 3 rows = ____ blocks altogether. 3 x 3 = ____

Pages 2-3

Pages 4-5

Pages 6-7

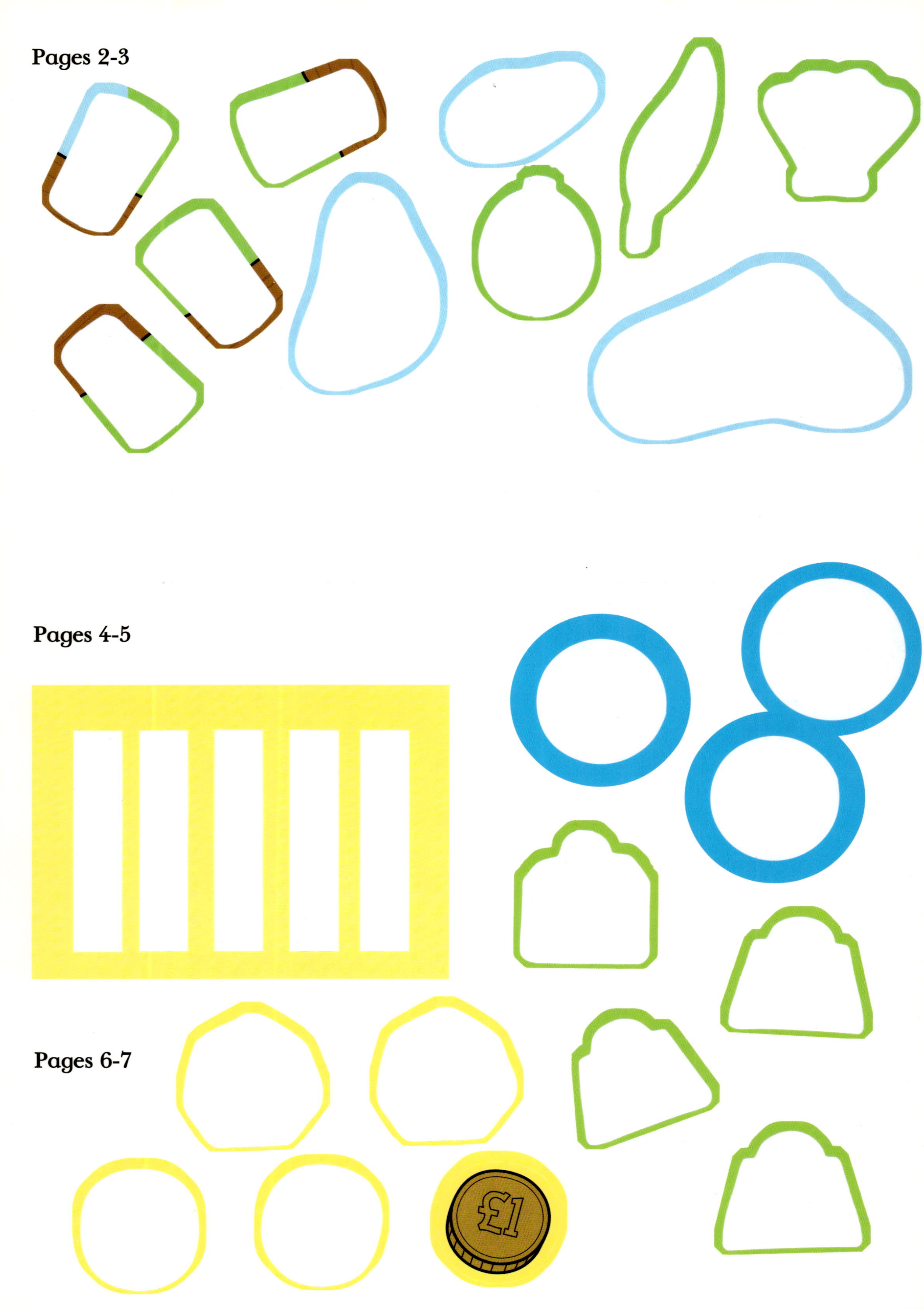

Pages 12-13

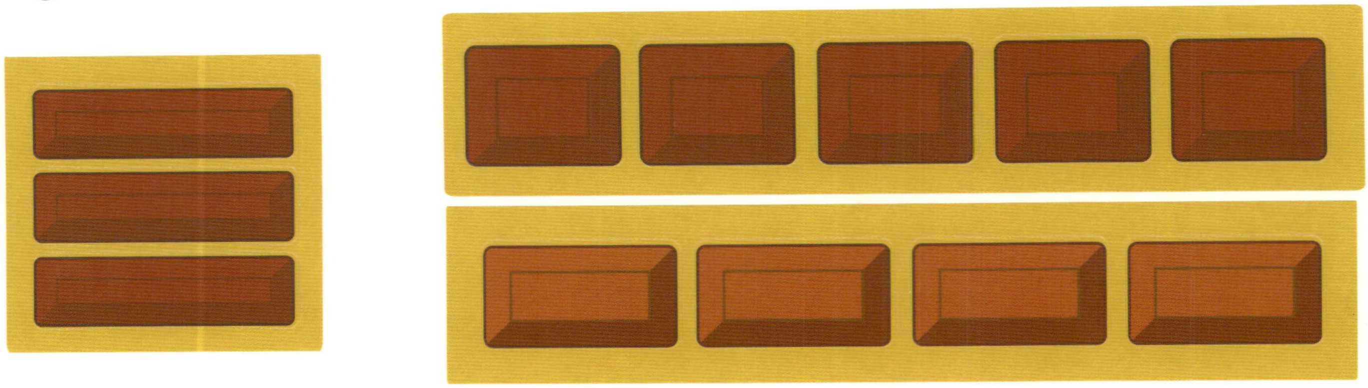

Pages 14-15

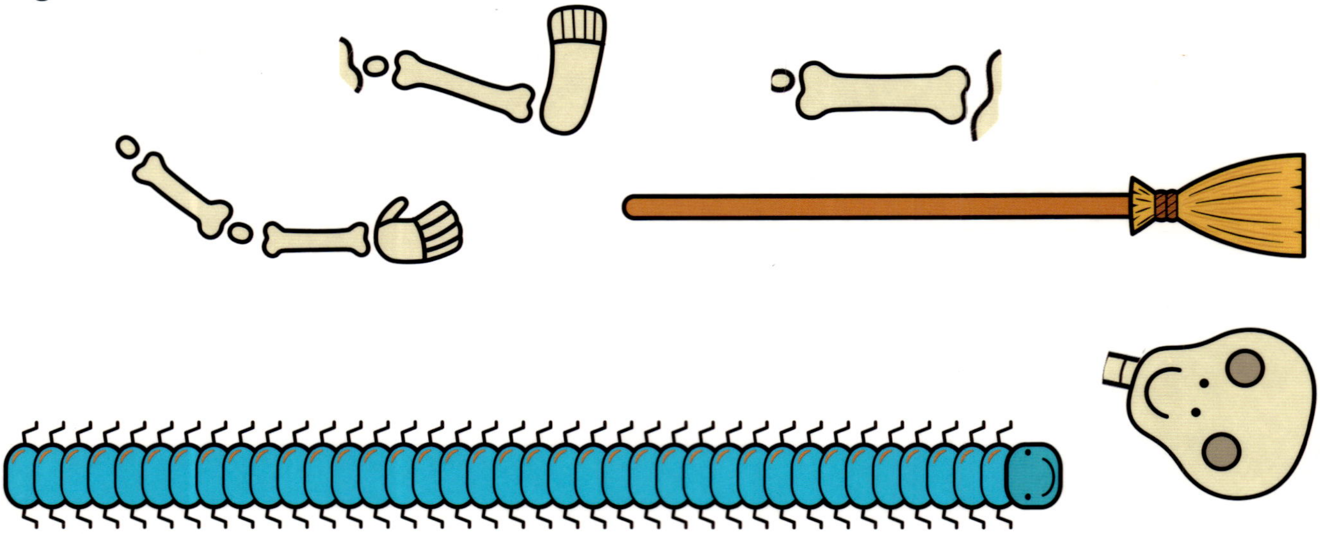

Pages 16-17

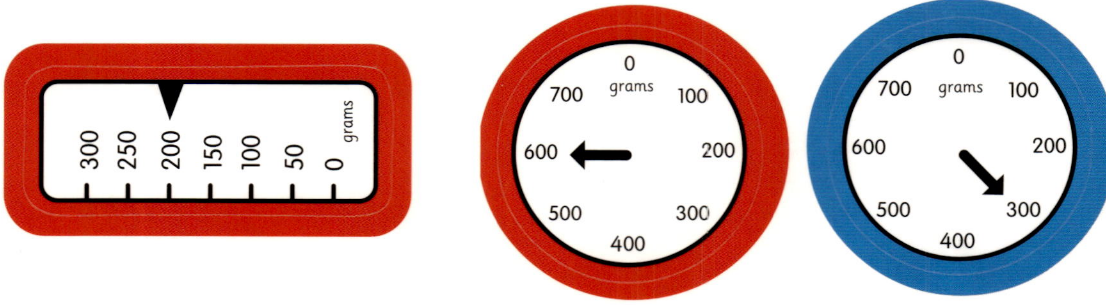

Pages 18-19

Pages 18-19

Pages 20-21

Pages 22-23

Reward chart stickers

Use these chunky chocolate bars to do these **division** questions.

10 ÷ 2 = ____

15 ÷ 3 = ____

16 ÷ 4 = ____

12 ÷ 3 = ____

Multiply

2 x 5 = ___

5 x 1 = ___

___ x 5 = 20

2 x 10 = ___

3 x ___ = 30

6 x 10 = ___

Divide

20 ÷ 10 = ___

15 ÷ ___ = 3

16 ÷ 2 = ___

10 ÷ ___ = 2

4 ÷ ___ = 2

8 ÷ 2 = ___

Measurement

Spooky centimetres

Find the sticker broomstick and stick it in the correct place.
Now **measure** it against this ruler. Write the **length** in the box.

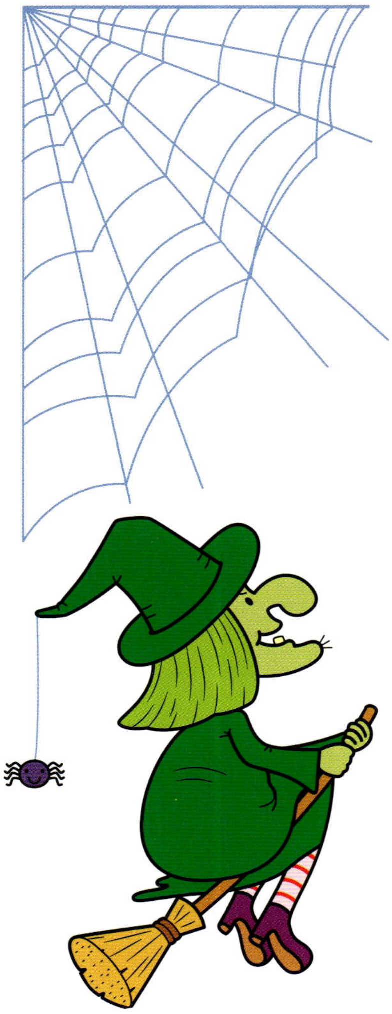

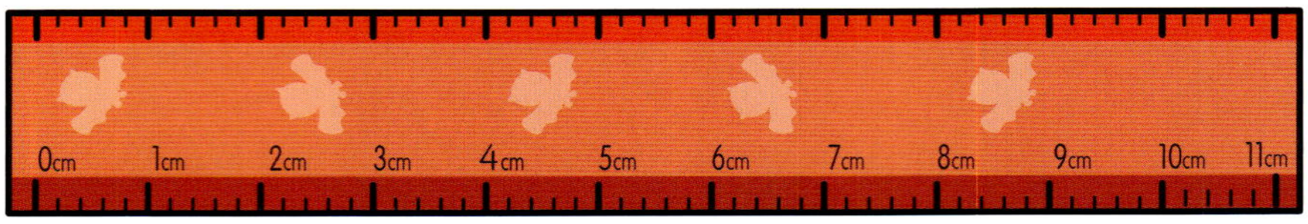

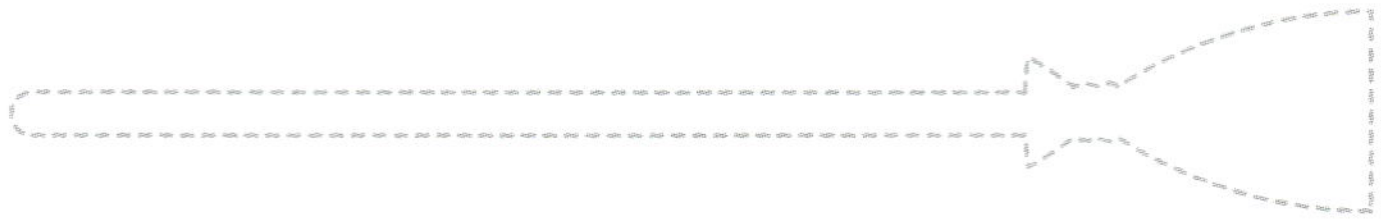

0cm
1cm
2cm
3cm
4cm
5cm
6cm
7cm
8cm
9cm
10cm
11cm

cm

Now draw your own broomstick and measure it.

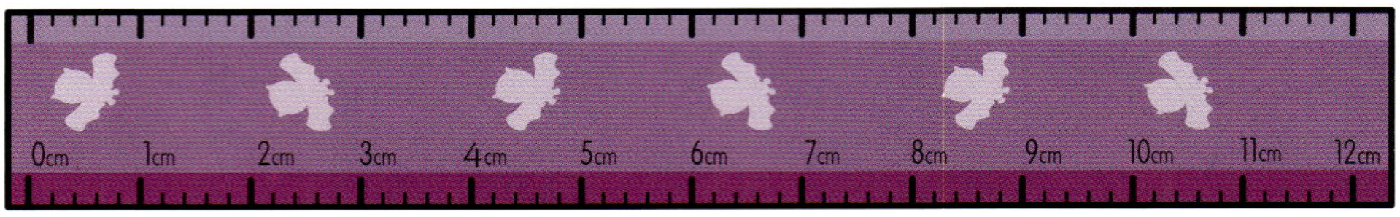

0cm
1cm
2cm
3cm
4cm
5cm
6cm
7cm
8cm
9cm
10cm
11cm
12cm

cm

Find a sticker of a centipede and stick it in the correct place. Now measure it against this ruler.

0cm
1cm
2cm
3cm
4cm
5cm
6cm
7cm
8cm
9cm
10cm
11cm
12cm
13cm
14cm

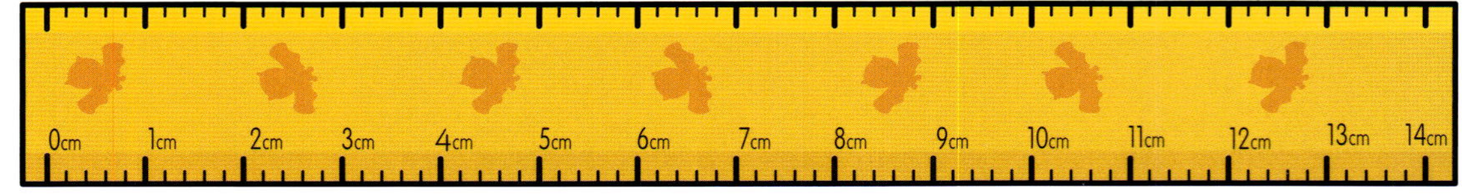

The centipede is _____ cm long.

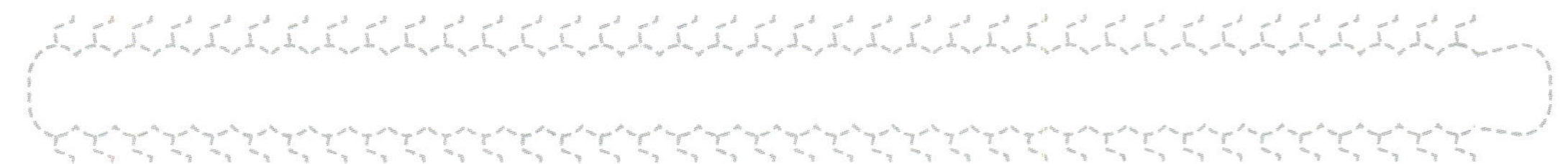

Sid the skeleton has been shrunk by Selma, the wicked witch!

Find his missing bones on your sticker sheet.

How **tall** is Sid?

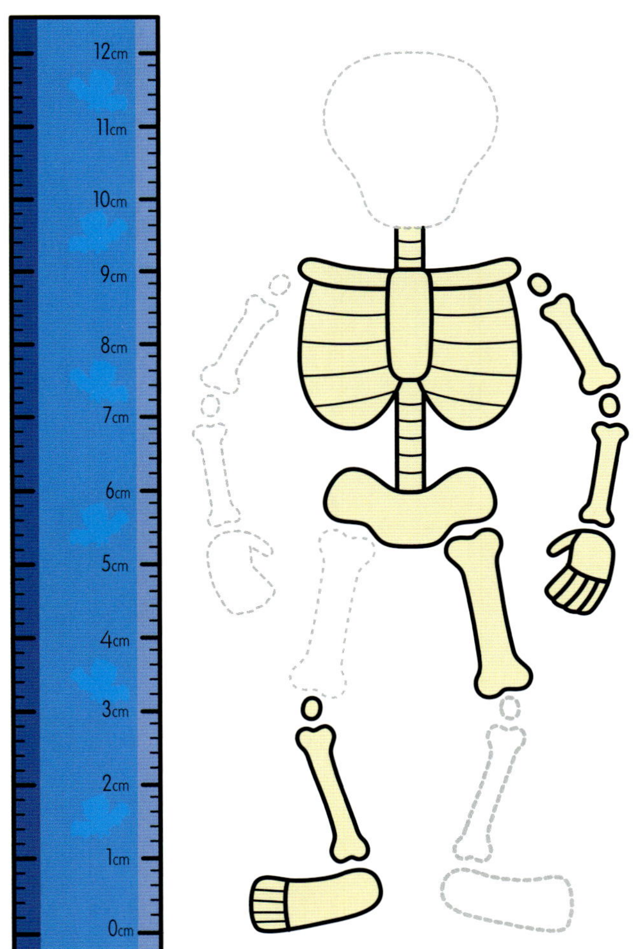

Sid is _____ cm tall.

Can you work out the missing numbers?

10cm + 10cm = _____

_____ + 10cm = 50cm

_____ + 20cm = 40cm

10cm + 20cm = _____

60cm + 30cm = _____

40cm - 20cm = _____

30cm - _____ = 20cm

50cm - _____ = 10cm

Answer these questions in metres and centimetres.

20cm + 80cm = __m

1m + 20cm = __m____cm

20cm + 120cm = __m____cm

80cm + 40cm = __m____cm

Reading scales

Silly science lab

Find a sticker scale which says the correct **weight.**

Baby dragon weighs **300g**

Asteroid weighs **200g**

Moon dust weighs **600g**

Colour each jug to show the correct **volume.**

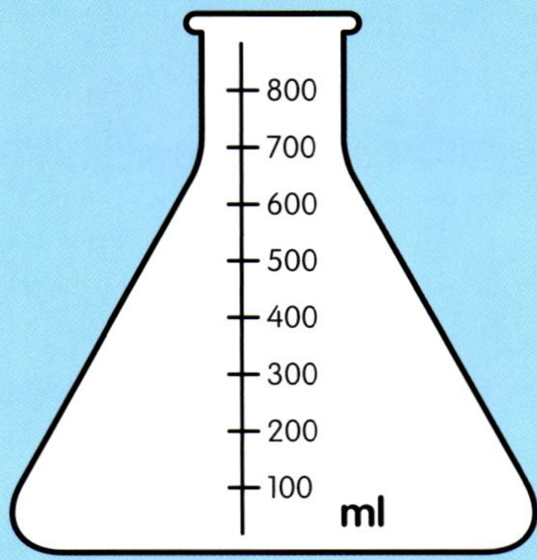

200ml of frogspawn

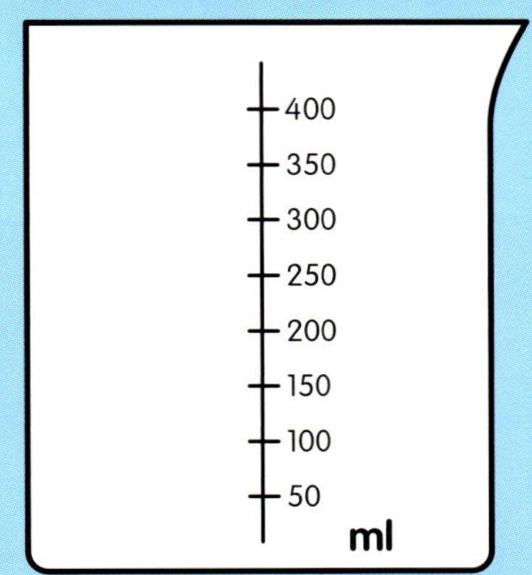

400ml of seawater

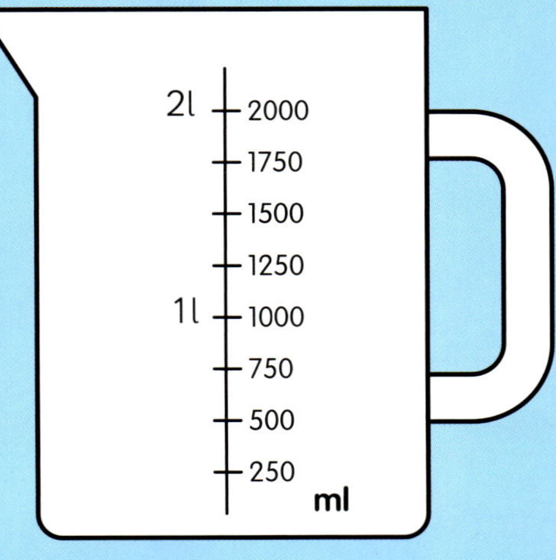

1l of peppermint tea

Read each scale and write the amount.

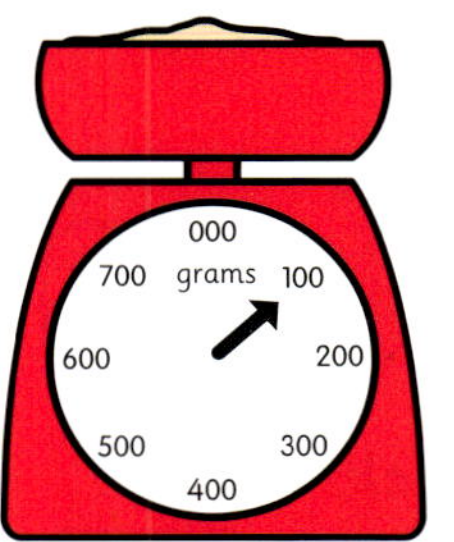

100g

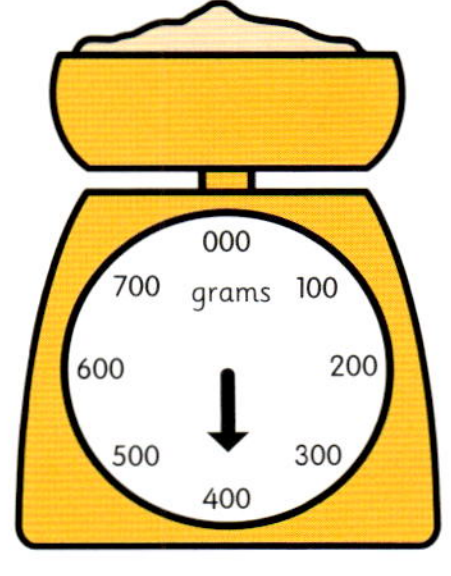

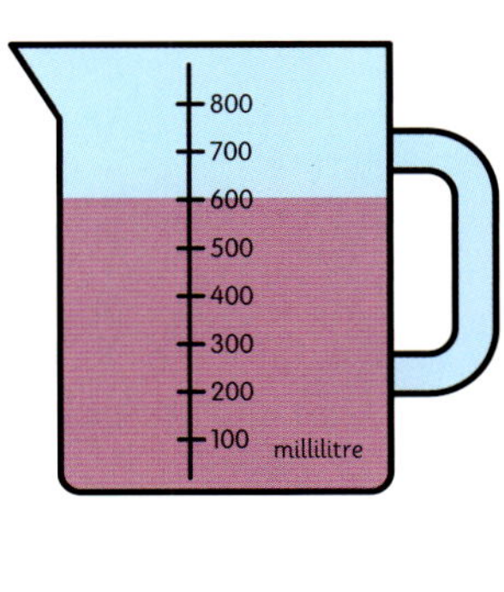

Pictograms

Ahoy there, pirates!

Find the treasure chests and stick them by the correct pirate's name.

Bluebeard

Blackjack

Skull

Bones

Which pirate has the least treasure? ______________

Which pirate has 5 chests? ______________

How many chests does Bones have? ______________

Which pirates have the same amount of treasure?

______________ and ______________

Shiver me timbers!

Use the clues below to stick the correct number of skull and crossbones stickers onto the chart. Each skull and crossbones stands for one battle.

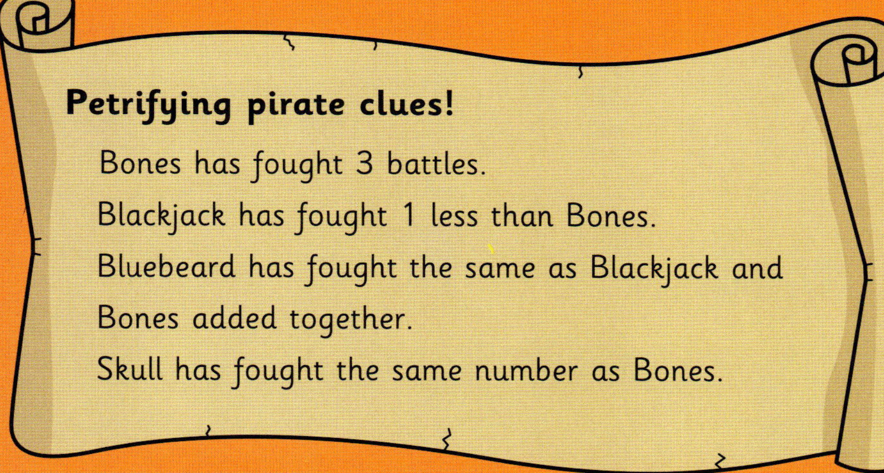

Petrifying pirate clues!

Bones has fought 3 battles.

Blackjack has fought 1 less than Bones.

Bluebeard has fought the same as Blackjack and Bones added together.

Skull has fought the same number as Bones.

Puzzles for pirates

1 pirate boat has 5 sails. How many sails do 2 boats have?

____

There are 16 pirates and half of them have an eye-patch. How many eye-patches are there?

____

2 pirates are sharing out 12 gold coins. How many do they have each?

____

1 ship has 4 cannons. How many cannons do 2 ships have?

____

Symmetry

A hive of activity

Use the bee stickers to make each hive **symmetrical**.

Draw the other side of the beehive to make it symmetrical.

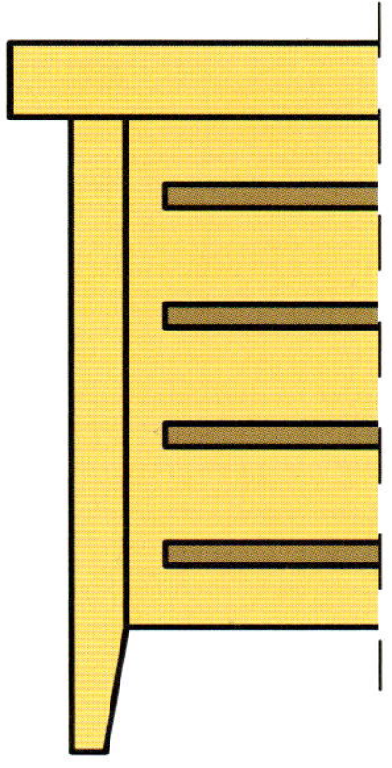

Complete the jar.

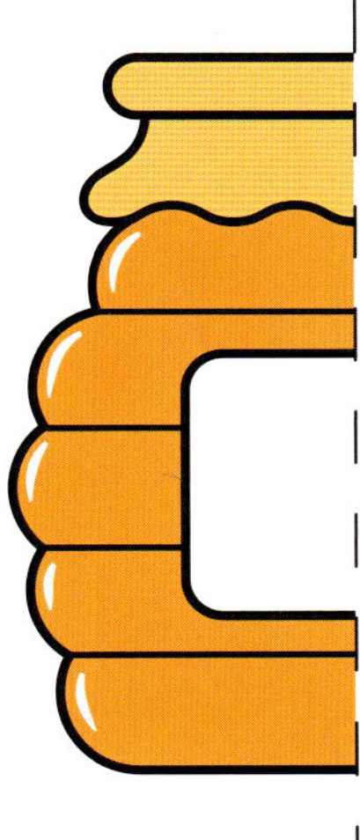

Complete the bumble bee and colour it.

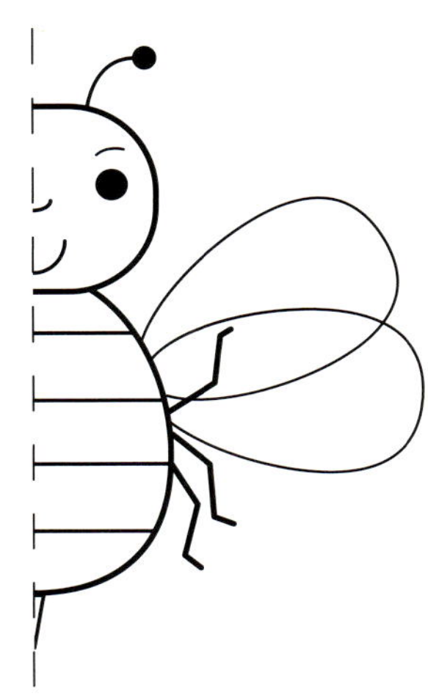

Shapes and sorting

Little shops of shapes

Each shop sells things of only one shape. Find some more things to stick in each of the shop windows.

SHOP OF

CONES

All shapes and sizes!

Count the tennis balls. Is there an even or an odd number?

____

If you were sharing the apples between 2 people, how many would each person get?

____

If you were sharing all the cones between 4 people, how many cones would each person get?

____

Is there an odd or an even number of cones?

____

Reward chart

Use this chart to keep a record of your progress. Each time you finish an activity, reward yourself with a star. How many can you collect?

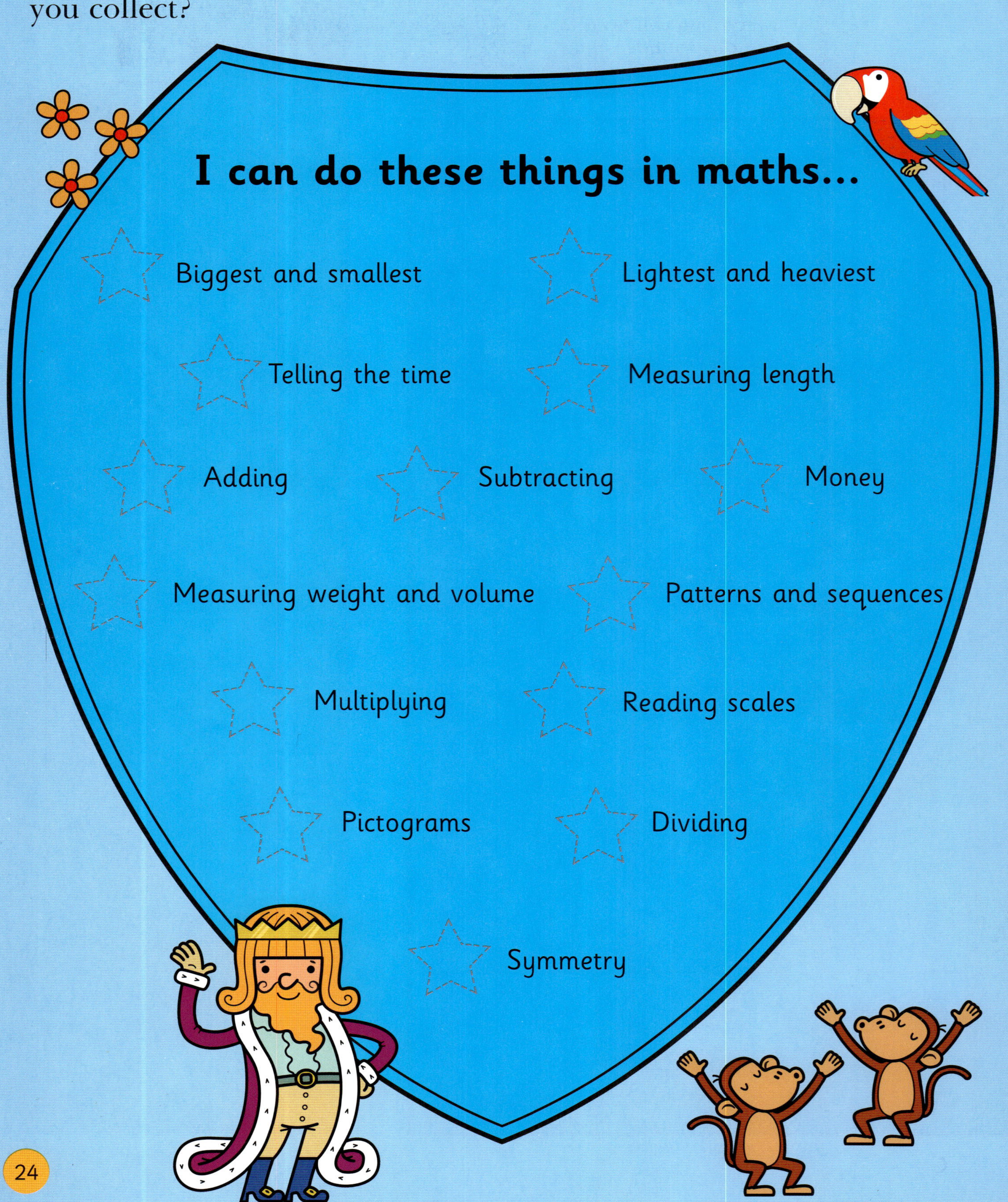